The Snow Goose and Other Stories

Paul Gallico

Level 3

Retold by John Escott

Series Editors: Andy Hopkins and Jocelyn Potter

Pearson Education Limited
Edinburgh Gate, Harlow,
Essex CM20 2JE, England
and Associated Companies throughout the world.

ISBN: 978-1-4058-5073-5

First edition published 2000
This edition published 2007

1 3 5 7 9 10 8 6 4 2

Text copyright © Penguin Books Ltd 2000
This edition copyright © Pearson Education Ltd 2007
Illustrations by Andrés Guerrero

Set in 11/13pt A. Garamond
Printed in China
SWTC/01

Produced for the Publishers by AC Estudio Editorial S.L.

Published by Pearson Education Ltd in association with Penguin Books Ltd,
both companies being subsidiaries of Pearson Plc.

Acknowledgements
We are grateful to the following for permission to reproduce photographs:

Corbis: page 75(c) (David James) (Warner Bros/ZUMA); **Getty Images:** page 75(f);
NHPA Ltd/Photoshot Holdings: page 28 (Snow Goose in flight) (Mike Lane);
The Picture Desk: page 75(d) (Avco Embassy), page 75(e) (Hal Roach/MGM) (The Kobal Collection)

Picture Research by Lisa Wren/Sandra Hilsdon

Every effort has been made to trace the copyright holders and we apologise in advance for any
unintentional omissions. We would be pleased to insert the appropriate acknowledgement
in any subsequent edition of this publication

Contents

1.1 What's the book about?

1 There are three stories in this book. Look at the pictures below. Guess which picture (1, 2, 3) is from each story.

a ☐ *The Snow Goose*: Philip helps a bird.

b ☐ *The Doll*: Doctor Amony buys a present for a little girl.

c ☐ *The Silver Swans*: Doctor Fundoby meets a young woman who lives on a boat.

2 When and where do the stories happen? Tick (✓) the correct answers.

a ☐ 1800 to 1900   ☐ 1930 to 1960   ☐ 2000 to 2010

b ☐ England   ☐ the US   ☐ South Africa

1.2 What happens first?

Look at the pictures on pages 1–11. What can you guess about Philip? Circle the correct words.

1 Philip loves *birds / parties*.

2 He lives by *a river / the sea*.

3 He is *an artist / a sailor*.

4 He is *handsome / kind*.

The Snow Goose

Women turned their eyes away when they saw him.
So they never learned that he was a lover of all living things.

The Great **Marsh** lies on the Essex coast, between the villages of Chelmbury and Wickaeldroth.

It is one of the last wild and lonely places in England. Nobody lives there. The only sounds are the cries of the many birds that make their homes in the marsh. It is a long, low, flat land of grass and water. Greys and blues and soft greens are the colours. But sometimes, when the sun goes down, the sky and land are a wonderful red and gold.

In the spring of 1930, a man bought some land and an old, empty **lighthouse** standing at the mouth of the little river Aelder. The man's name was Philip Rhayader. He lived and worked alone at the lighthouse all through the year. He was a painter, and he painted pictures of the birds and the marsh.

marsh /mɑːʃ/ (n) an area of soft, wet land
lighthouse /ˈlaɪthaʊs/ (n) a tall building with a bright light that tells ships about dangerous rocks

Philip lived at the lighthouse because he wanted to live alone. Every two weeks he went to the village of Chelmbury for the food and other things that he needed. When the villagers first saw the strange shape of his body and his dark, bearded face, they were a little afraid of him. They spoke of him as 'that strange painter-man from the lighthouse'. But slowly, as time passed, they learned to accept his strange ways.

Philip was a **hunchback**. His left arm was weak and thin and **twisted**, and his left hand looked like a bird's foot. He was twenty-seven when he came to the lighthouse on the Great Marsh.

He lived in many places before he came there. He always tried hard to make friends with the people that he met. But other people did not want to be friends with Philip. His twisted body made them uncomfortable. Women turned their eyes away when they saw him. So they never learned that he was a **gentle** man and a lover of all living things.

Philip did not hate these people. His heart was too full of love; he could only feel sadness for them.

hunchback /ˈhʌntʃbæk/ (n) an impolite word for a person with a thick, hard part on their back, or with a very rounded back
twisted /ˈtwɪstɪd/ (adj) strangely turned into a shape that is not normal
gentle /ˈdʒentl/ (adj) calm and kind

He spent time with his birds and his paintings. He owned a sailing boat and he could sail very well in it. He sailed up and down the rivers, and sometimes out to sea. Often he went away for many days. He looked for different birds to draw and photograph, and then to paint.

He built an **enclosure** at the side of the lighthouse, and sometimes he caught birds and put them in there. He never shot at a bird. If someone shot at them, he told them not to come near the lighthouse. He was a friend to all living things, and so all living things became his friends.

Some of the birds in the enclosure were the **geese** that flew down the coast from Iceland and Spitzbergen each October. They filled the air with the noise of their **wings**. Many hundreds came and stayed with him through the cold weather, from October to the early spring. Then they flew north again. But they came back in the autumn. Something inside them knew that Philip's place was a safe place for the winter.

And this made Philip happy.

◆

enclosure /ɪnˈkləʊʒə/ (n) an area with something like a wall around it
goose /guːs/ (n) a large water bird with a long neck that makes a loud noise
wing /wɪŋ/ (n) one of the two parts of a bird's body that it uses for flying

One November afternoon, three years after Philip came to the Great Marsh, a girl came to the door of the lighthouse with something in her arms. She was twelve years old, thin and untidy. She had fair hair and blue eyes.

She was afraid to knock at the door. People told strange stories about the man who lived in the lighthouse. But her reason for being here was more important than her fear. In one of the stories about him, the villagers said, 'This hunchback man at the lighthouse can make hurt or sick birds better.'

The girl knocked at the door and waited. Slowly, the door opened. When she saw Philip, with his thick hair and beard, she nearly ran away. But then he spoke. He had a kind voice.

'What do you want, little girl?' he asked gently.

She pushed out her arms towards him. In them was a large, white bird. The bird did not move. There was blood on its **feather**s and more blood on the front of her dress. She gave the bird to him.

'I found it,' she said, quietly.

'Did you?' he said.

'Yes,' she said. 'It's hurt.'

'I can see that,' he said.

'Is it still alive?' she asked.

'Yes. Yes, I think so,' he said, looking at it. 'Come in, child, come in.'

Philip went inside, carrying the bird. The girl still felt afraid but she followed him. She wanted to see inside the lighthouse. He put the bird carefully on to the table. The room was warm; a fire was burning. There were many pictures on the wall, and the room was full of a strange but pleasant smell.

The bird moved, and Philip gently opened one of its large white wings. It was black at the end.

He turned to the girl. 'Where did you find it?' he asked.

'There's a place in the marsh where the men shoot birds,' she said. 'What sort of bird is it?'

'It's a snow goose from Canada,' he told her. Then he said to himself, in surprise: 'But why is it here?'

'Can you make it better?' asked the girl.

'Yes, yes,' said Philip. 'We'll try. You can help.'

Philip put the things that he needed on the table. His gentle hands began to work on the bird, and the child watched with wide-open eyes.

'She was shot, poor thing,' he said.

'Oh!' she said.

feather /ˈfeðə/ (n) one of the light, soft things that cover a bird's body

4

'One of her legs is broken, and the end of the wing,' he said. 'But not badly. We must cover the part of the wing that is hurt. Then, in the spring, the feathers will grow and she'll be able to fly again.'

As he worked, he told her a wonderful story.

'She's only a young snow goose, you know – about a year old. She comes from Canada. That's a big country far, far away across the ocean. In Canada the winters are very, very cold, so each year the snow geese fly south to warmer countries. But this time, as this snow goose was flying south, she flew into a great storm.

'It was a wild, wild storm, and the wind picked her up and carried her with it for many days and nights. She had strong wings, but they could not help her. At last the storm ended and she was able to fly south again.

'But now she was flying over England – a strange place to her, with strange birds. She was lost and tired, so she landed here in the friendly green marsh. And when she came down to rest, did we greet her like a visiting princess? No! A man with a gun tried to shoot her!'

He put a thin piece of wood on the broken leg to hold it straight. While he was mending the bird's leg, he told her about the birds in his enclosure.

'The geese in the enclosure flew all the way from Iceland and Spitzbergen,' he told her. 'They arrive in October. They make the sky dark because there are so many of them. The sound of their wings is like a strong wind.'

He finished mending the leg. Then they went outside and put the snow goose with the other birds. As he placed her gently in the enclosure, Philip said, 'In a few days she'll be much better. We'll call her the Lost Princess.'

The girl looked pleased. Then she noticed that some of the birds were unable to fly.

'What's the matter with those birds?' she asked. She pointed at two birds who were trying to fly.

'I've cut the ends of their wings,' he said, 'so they can't fly. They have to stay here.'

'Does it hurt them?' she asked.

'No, no, little girl,' he said, laughing gently. 'The feathers will grow again next spring.'

'So why do you cut their wings?' she asked.

'Because these birds will show the others that there's food here. It's a safe place for them to stay,' he answered her. 'In the spring, they'll fly back to their homes in the north.'

While she listened to him, she forgot the strange stories about him. But suddenly she remembered them and ran to the path towards the village.

Philip called after her. 'What's your name?'

She stopped running and turned to answer him.

'It's Fritha,' she called back.

'Where do you live?' he asked.

'With the fishing people in the village,' she replied.

'Will you come back in a day or two? You can see how the Princess is,' he said.

She did not answer immediately, but at last he heard her say, 'Yes.'

Then she ran along the path.

◆

The snow goose got better very quickly. By the middle of winter, she was able to walk about in the enclosure with the other birds. Fritha often walked to the lighthouse to see the Princess. At each visit her fear of Philip became less and less. She loved Philip's story about this strange, white princess. He showed her a map of Canada, the goose's home.

Then, one morning in June, the Princess left them.

Fritha was at the lighthouse at the time. She saw the great bird flying in wider and wider circles, up into the sky. Her white wings shone in the spring sun.

'Look!' Fritha shouted to Philip. 'Look at the Princess! Is she leaving us?'

Philip came running from his painting. The snow goose got smaller and smaller in the sky, and finally disappeared.

'Yes, the Princess is going home,' he said quietly. 'Listen, she's saying goodbye.'

As they stood listening, the sad call of the snow goose came through the air.

Fritha did not come to the lighthouse after the snow goose left. Philip was alone again with his birds and his paintings.

That summer, from his memory, he painted a picture of a thin, untidy little girl with fair hair. The girl was carrying a big white bird.

◆

It was October again and Philip was in the enclosure. He was feeding the birds that could not fly. The cold northeast wind and the noise from the sea made it hard to hear any other sounds. Suddenly Philip heard the high, clear call of a bird. He turned his head and looked into the sky.

At first he could only see something small. But as it came closer, it grew into the shape of a bird. While Philip watched, the bird flew round the lighthouse. Then it dropped into the enclosure. His eyes filled with tears. It was the snow goose!

Philip watched her walk round the enclosure.

'She acts like a bird that's never been away!' he said to himself. But he did not understand. 'How could she go all the way home to Canada and then come back here again?' he thought. 'Perhaps she spent the summer in Greenland. Then it was time to fly south again. She remembered our kindness and returned.'

Philip immediately thought of Fritha. He knew that he must tell her. So when he went to the village for food, he left a note at the post office. It said:

Tell Fritha (of the fishing people) that the Princess is back.

Three days later Fritha came to the lighthouse to visit the Lost Princess. The girl was taller but still untidy.

◆

The years passed. On the Great Marsh very little changed. The sea continued to move in and out, and the birds came and went with the seasons. For Philip the coming and going of the snow goose showed the passing of time.

When the snow goose was at the lighthouse, Fritha visited Philip. She sailed with him in his boat and they caught birds for the enclosure. Fritha learned many things from Philip. He taught her everything about the wild birds that flew across the marshes. She learned how to get his paints ready. Sometimes she cooked a meal for him.

But when the snow goose left in the summer, Fritha did not come to the lighthouse. She did not feel that she could visit Philip. The bird was not there.

Then, one year, the Princess did not return. Philip was very sad and lonely. He spent all his time painting. He painted all winter and through the next summer. He did not see Fritha.

But in October he heard again the cry of the snow goose. And the beautiful white bird, bigger than before, dropped from the sky.

'She came back!' he said happily.

Philip went into the village immediately. As before, he left a note at the post office for Fritha.

This time it was a month before she came to the lighthouse. When he saw her, he was surprised. She was grown-up; she was not a child now.

From that time, the snow goose stayed at the lighthouse for longer and longer each year. She followed Philip everywhere outside. Sometimes she went into the lighthouse when he was working.

And so time passed ...

2.1 Were you right?

Look back at your answers to Activity 1.2 on page iv. Then complete this information.

Name	Philip Rhayader
Home	
Job	
Words that describe him	

2.2 What more did you learn?

Complete the sentences with one of these:

| Fritha | the Princess | Philip |

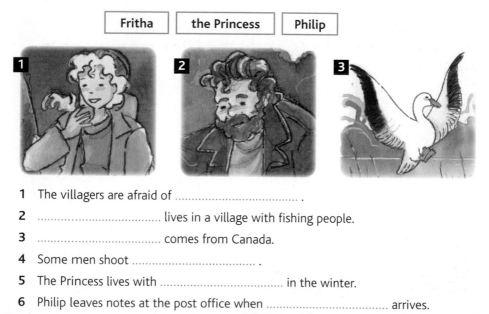

1 The villagers are afraid of ....

2 .... lives in a village with fishing people.

3 .... comes from Canada.

4 Some men shoot ....

5 The Princess lives with .... in the winter.

6 Philip leaves notes at the post office when .... arrives.

2.3 Language in use

**Look at the sentences on the right.
Then join these sentences in
the same way.**

> Philip went inside, **carrying** the bird.
> 'No, no, little girl,' he said, **laughing**
> gently.

1 Philip lived quietly. He stayed away from other people.

   Philip lived quietly, staying away from other people.

2 He often went away in his boat. He was looking for interesting birds.

   ....

3 The girl knocked at the door. She was holding the bird in her arms.

   ....

4 'She'll be OK,' said Philip. He was mending the bird's leg.

   ....

5 'I'll come back soon,' said Fritha. She was smiling.

   ....

6 The Princess was leaving. She flew higher and higher.

   ....

2.4 What's next?

**The story ends in 1940. What do you think? Tick (✓) one or more answers to
each question.**

1 Which of these will be important to the story?

   love ☐   boats ☐   war ☐   family ☐

2 Who and/or what is still fine at the end of the story?

The Snow Goose

*Fritha looked at Philip. He was changed. For the first
time he was not ugly, but very beautiful.*

In the spring of 1940, the birds left the Great Marsh early and flew away to their summer homes in the north. Something was happening in the world outside the Great Marsh. That something changed the lives of Philip, Fritha and the snow goose.

It was the Second World War.

On the first day of May, Philip and Fritha watched as the last birds left the enclosure. The snow goose started to fly away too. But she did not fly with the others. She just flew around their heads a few times and landed back in the enclosure.

'She isn't going!' said Fritha, surprised. 'The Princess is staying.'

'Yes,' said Philip.

His voice was shaking, because he, too, was surprised.

'She'll stay here now,' he said. 'She'll never fly away again. The Lost Princess isn't lost now. She's decided to stay. This will be her home now.'

As he spoke these words, Philip thought: 'And Fritha comes and goes from the lighthouse. She's like the snow goose. But I like it when she comes. Her visits make me happy.'

Philip looked at Fritha. She was a young woman now.

And suddenly he knew that he loved her.

But he could not tell Fritha about his love for her. He did not frighten her now. He knew that. But it was unpleasant for her to look at him. He knew that too. So his loving words for her stayed locked in his heart. But his loving feelings towards her showed clearly in his eyes.

Fritha turned to Philip when he finished speaking. She could see that he was lonely. But she could also see a look in his eyes that she could not understand. The sadness and gentleness in them made her unhappy inside herself. She could not find any words to say to him. She looked away.

For some minutes neither of them spoke.

At last Fritha said, 'I ... I must go. I'm glad that the Princess is staying. Now you won't be so lonely.'

She walked away from him quickly, and only half-heard him say sadly, 'Goodbye, Fritha.'

When she was far away, she stopped. She turned and she looked back at the lighthouse. He was still standing in the same place, watching her. After a minute or two, she turned towards the village and walked slowly home, away from the lighthouse and the man outside it.

◆

It was a little more than three weeks before Fritha returned to the lighthouse. By then it was the end of May. She wanted to know if the snow goose really did stay at the lighthouse. She came in the early evening, when the moon was already in the eastern sky.

She saw a yellow light shining from the place where Philip kept his boat. She hurried down to the river.

The boat was moving gently from side to side in the water. Philip was putting drinking water, food, clothes and another sail into it. He heard her coming and turned round. His face was pale but his dark eyes were excited.

Fritha saw what he was doing. She immediately forgot about the snow goose. 'Philip! Are you going away?' she asked.

He stopped working to greet her. She saw from the look of excitement in his eyes that he was doing something very urgent and important.

'Fritha! I'm glad that you've come,' he said. 'Yes, I must go away. A little journey.'

'A journey?' she said.

'Yes,' he said. 'I'll come back when I can.'

'Where must you go?' she asked.

His words poured out now.

'I must go to Dunkirk, 160 kilometres across the Channel,' he said. 'British soldiers are waiting there on the beaches – waiting to die. The Germans are moving nearer and nearer all the time.'

'How do you know this?' she asked.

'I heard about it when I was in the village,' he said. 'The British can't move. They have the sea in front of them, and the German soldiers behind them. Dunkirk is on fire. There's little hope for them. The government in London has asked everyone with a boat to sail across the Channel. They want us to take as many soldiers as possible off the beaches. They want us to take them out to the big boats in the deeper water.'

'And you are going,' said Fritha.

'Yes,' said Philip. 'I'm going to take my little boat across the Channel, Fritha. I must. I can take six men, perhaps seven, each time I sail from the beach to one of the large ships. Do you understand now that I have to go?'

Fritha was a simple country girl who did not understand about war. She did not know what was happening to the soldiers on the beaches of France. She only knew that this journey was dangerous for Philip. She was afraid.

'Philip, must you go?' she cried.

'Yes,' he said softly. 'I must.'

'You won't come back!' she cried. 'Why must it be you?'

Philip began to speak gently to her. There was no excitement in his voice now. He explained why he had to help the men at Dunkirk. He spoke slowly, because he wanted her to understand.

'Those soldiers are like the birds that we've helped here,' he said. 'Many of them are hurt, like the Lost Princess who you brought to me. They are afraid, and they need help, my dear, like the birds. I can do something for them.' He smiled. 'At last I can be a man and help in this terrible war.'

Fritha looked at Philip. He was changed. For the first time she saw that he was not ugly, but very beautiful. She wanted to tell him this, but she could not

find the words. She remembered the look that she saw in his eyes a few weeks before. Now she knew what it was.

It was love.

Suddenly she cried, 'I'll go with you, Philip!'

Philip shook his head. 'No,' he said. 'If you come, you'll take a soldier's place in the boat. Do you understand? No, I must go alone.'

He put on a rubber coat and boots, and climbed into the boat. 'Goodbye, Fritha,' he said. 'Look after the birds until I return to the lighthouse.'

As he sailed away, he turned. He waved to her. She waved back, but she was unhappy.

'I'll look after them, Philip,' she replied.

It was night now. The moon was bright, and there were stars in the sky. Fritha watched the boat sail out to sea. Suddenly, from the darkness behind her, came the sound of wings. Something flew past her into the air! Fritha looked up and saw the snow goose flying into the night sky. It went round the lighthouse once, then it flew out to sea – after Philip's boat. When it reached the little boat, it flew above it in slow, wide circles.

'Look after him, Princess!' called Fritha.

She watched the white sail and the white bird for a long time. Then, at last, they disappeared into the night. Fritha turned and walked slowly back to the empty lighthouse.

◆

The rest of the story about Philip Rhayader and the snow goose is in two parts. A soldier – Private Potton – tells one part.

Private Potton was with the first 200 soldiers who arrived home from Dunkirk. A boat carried them across the Channel. Newspaper reporters from *The Times*, the *Evening News*, the *Daily Sketch* and the *Daily Express* were waiting for them when they arrived in England.

The reporters came from London. They wanted the story of the men's escape from Dunkirk, but many of the soldiers were hurt, or they were too tired to talk to the reporters.

But not Private Potton. He went with some others to a pub and was happy to tell his story to everyone. And the reporters were very happy to listen. They wrote down every word that he said.

Suddenly one of them asked: 'What do you mean ... "it was hopeless"?'

Potton turned to answer him. 'Listen. There we were, on that beach, with no place to go to. The Germans were behind us and the sea was in front of us. That's right, isn't it, Jock? Jock was there, too.'

The man next to Potton said, 'Yes, that's right.'

'The shooting came at us from all sides ... from the air, too, as the planes flew low over the beaches,' continued Potton. 'We all lay on that beach and put our hands over our heads. The noise was terrible! You couldn't hear yourself speak, could you, Jock?'

'That's right,' said Jock.

'There was smoke everywhere,' continued Potton. 'It was so thick at times – you could almost taste it. And out at sea we could hear the fighting between the German planes and the British warships.

'We waited for them to hit us. We were too sick and tired to move. And less than a kilometre out at sea was the boat, the *Kentish Maid*. I know that boat well. She always sailed out from Margate in the summer. I've been on her, many times, when I was on holiday in Margate. Well, there she was, waiting to take us home to dear old England. But we couldn't swim out to her, and she couldn't come in nearer to us.

'Then suddenly, through the smoke, this goose came. Yes, a goose! I couldn't believe my eyes. But Jock saw it too, didn't you, Jock?'

'I did,' said Jock. 'It was white and it went round and round in circles above our heads.'

'Jock shouted out, "It means death for all of us",' said Potton. 'But I shouted back, "It means good luck." Then through the thick smoke comes the man – sailing in this little boat.'

'What man?' asked a reporter from *The Times*.

'The man who saved us!' said Private Potton. 'He came sailing near the beach. He took no notice of the guns and **bomb**s. In he sailed, like a man out sailing on a Sunday afternoon!

'But he was a strange-looking man, wasn't he, Jock?'

'Strange, yes,' said Jock.

'He had a beard, a thin and twisted left arm, and a hunched back,' continued Potton. 'He was guiding the boat with his good hand.

'He waved us out to his boat and shouted to our officer, "I can take seven men at a time!" Our officer thanked him and told the nearest seven of us to get in.

'Jock and I were two of those seven, so we pushed through the water to the boat. But it was hard work, even that short way, wasn't it, Jock?'

'Yes,' said Jock. 'When we reached the boat we were so tired. We couldn't even climb over the side. But the man was strong, and he pulled us in.'

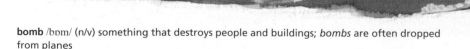

bomb /bɒm/ (n/v) something that destroys people and buildings; *bombs* are often dropped from planes

'He told us to lie in the bottom of the boat,' said Potton. 'Then we sailed away. When I looked at the sail I was surprised. How did the boat move? The sail was full of holes from the shooting!

'And up there, over our heads, that goose flew round and round and round. Never stopped, did it, Jock?'

'No,' said Jock.

'"There, that goose *does* mean good luck!" I said to Jock. When the man heard me, at the back of the boat, he looked up at the goose. And he smiled. "He knows her!" I thought to myself.

'We got to the *Kentish Maid* and climbed up on her. Then the man and the goose turned round and went back to the beach for seven more soldiers. He made journeys all afternoon and all night, too. He could see at night because Dunkirk was on fire: it lit up the sky! I don't know how many journeys he made. He was very tired. But he didn't stop, did he, Jock?'

'He didn't,' said Jock.

The Snow Goose and Other Stories

'There was also a large boat from the Thames Sailing Club and a big boat from Poole. Those two boats brought all of us off that beach without losing a man.

'The *Kentish Maid* sailed when the last man was off the beach. There were more than 700 of us on a boat that was built for 200.

'The man was still there when we left. He waved goodbye to us and then sailed off towards Dunkirk – that goose with him. Ooh – it was strange to see that big goose flying round and round the little sailing boat.

'We don't know who he was. We don't know what happened to him. But he was a good man, he was. He saved our lives, didn't he, Jock?'

'He did,' said Jock.

◆

Commander Keith Emerson also helped British soldiers escape from Dunkirk. At an officers' club in Brook Street, London, he told his story.

At four o'clock one morning, the telephone woke him, and someone asked him to take a boat across the Channel to Dunkirk. The slow but strong boat pulled four big Thames river boats along behind it. With these boats, the commander crossed the Channel many times to save the soldiers on the beaches.

'Did you hear that strange story about a wild goose?' one of the commander's friends asked. 'They were telling the story up and down the beaches, and some of the returning men were talking about it. They said, "It came between Dunkirk and La Panne. If you see it, you'll be safe."'

'Hmm,' said the commander, 'a wild goose, you say? I saw a white goose and it was lucky for us, too. I'll tell you about it.

'We were on our way back from Dunkirk. It was our third journey back. At about six o'clock we saw a small sailing boat. There seemed to be a man or a body in it – and this white goose was standing on one of the sides. I decided to have a look. When we got nearer, I saw a man lying in the bottom of the boat – a man with a beard. The poor man was dead – shot many times.

'When we were next to the boat, one of my men tried to put his hand on the side. But the goose hit him with her wings. He couldn't get near.

'Suddenly one of the men with me shouted and pointed to something in the water. It was a **mine**! It was lucky for us that we went to look at that boat. That's why I'm not dead now!

'When all our boats were past the mine, our men shot at it. There was a very loud BANG! We looked for the sailing boat, but it wasn't there. It went down

commander /kəˈmɑːndə/ (n) an officer who is the head of a group of soldiers
mine /maɪn/ (n) something dangerous that is hidden underground; when you pass over a *mine*, it can kill you

when the mine went off. I'm afraid that the man went with his boat. The goose was in the air. She was flying round in circles above the place where the boat went down. She flew round three times, like someone saying goodbye. Then she flew away to the west. It was very strange and a little sad,' said the commander, as he finished his story.

◆

After Philip went to France, Fritha stayed at the lighthouse on the Great Marsh. She looked after the birds that could not fly away. She was waiting for something. But she did not know what she was waiting for. During the first days after Philip left, she watched at the sea wall for his boat. But the days passed and Philip did not return. She spent some days looking in the rooms of the lighthouse. In one room she found Philip's paintings. There were pictures of that wild and empty country around the lighthouse, and of the beautiful birds that came there.

And there was a painting of Fritha. She was still a child in the picture. It was her first day at the lighthouse, and she was standing at the lighthouse door. She held the snow goose in her arms.

'It's strange,' Fritha thought. 'This is the only painting of the snow goose. The only picture of the lost, wild bird that brought Philip and me together.'

It was a beautiful picture. Fritha could feel the love that went into the painting of it.

◆

Long before the snow goose circled the lighthouse with a last goodbye, Fritha knew. Philip was not coming back.

She was standing by the lighthouse one evening when she heard the bird's call. She ran to the sea wall and looked up into the red eastern sky. She saw the snow goose and looked down the river towards the sea. But she already knew that there was no hope. There was no little sailing boat. The snow goose was alone.

Then Fritha knew that she loved Philip. Tears filled her eyes and poured down her face. As she watched the snow goose, she could hear Philip's voice. It seemed to call to her, 'Fritha, Fritha, my love. Goodbye, my love.'

'I love you, Philip,' Fritha said to herself.

Fritha waited for the snow goose to land in the enclosure. The other birds sent up welcoming calls to her. She came down very low, but she flew up again into the sky. She circled the lighthouse once and then climbed higher into the sky.

Fritha watched the snow goose. She did not see it as a bird. She saw it as Philip's last goodbye before he disappeared for ever.

She put out her arms, high into the sky, and cried: 'Goodbye, Philip! Goodbye!'

She stopped crying. Then she watched in silence for a long time after the snow goose disappeared. At last she went into the lighthouse and found Philip's picture of her and the snow goose. She held it to her chest and walked home slowly along the old sea wall.

◆

Each night, for many weeks after that, Fritha went to the lighthouse. She fed the birds that could not fly. Then, early one morning, a German aeroplane flew over the lighthouse. The pilot made a mistake. He thought that he had to bomb the lighthouse. The plane flew high into the sky and then down towards the lighthouse. It dropped its bombs. After a minute there was nothing there. The lighthouse, and everything in it, was destroyed.

Fritha came in the evening to feed the birds. She was walking along the path and stopped suddenly. Where was the lighthouse? Where was the enclosure? The sea covered the place where the lighthouse stood the day before.

3.1 Were you right?

Look back at your answers to Activity 2.4. Then complete this description.

BOOK REVIEW

The Snow Goose and Other Stories

by Paul Gallico

The Snow Goose is the story of the
(1) ....
between two people who are first brought together by the needs of a wild bird. In a sad end to the story, Philip goes away in his
(2) ....
to the (3).............................

in France.
(4) ....
is killed, and a few weeks later the
(5) ....
is destroyed.

PENGUIN ACTIVE READING   LEVEL 3

The Snow Goose and Other Stories
Paul Gallico

3.2 What more did you learn?

Match the thoughts with the people. Then put them in the right order.

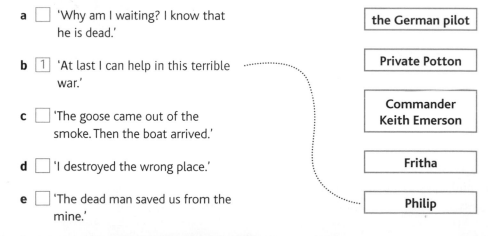

a ☐ 'Why am I waiting? I know that he is dead.'

b 1 'At last I can help in this terrible war.'

c ☐ 'The goose came out of the smoke. Then the boat arrived.'

d ☐ 'I destroyed the wrong place.'

e ☐ 'The dead man saved us from the mine.'

the German pilot

Private Potton

Commander Keith Emerson

Fritha

Philip

3.3 Language in use

Look at the sentences on the right. Then complete these sentences in the same way. Use past simple verb forms.

> They were **too** tired **to** talk to the reporters.
> We were **too** sick **to** move.

1 When the snow goose didn't leave, Fritha and Philip / surprised / speak .

   Fritha and Philip were too surprised to speak ....

2 When Philip left, Fritha / shy / talk about her love for him.

   ....

3 On the beach at Dunkirk, it / smoky / see clearly.

   ....

4 Near the beach, the water / shallow / sail a large ship.

   ....

5 When Philip was dead, the snow goose / afraid / let the soldiers onto the boat.

   ....

6 When the snow goose said goodbye, Fritha / sad / talk to anyone about Philip.

   ....

3.4 What's next?

Look at the pictures in the first part of the next story.

What do you think the story is about? Make notes.

Notes

The Doll

I remembered Jim's description of the woman who made her.
How could a woman like that make a beautiful doll?

My name is Stephen Amony and I am a doctor. I live and work in London, and I have a house by the river Thames. Everything in this story happened because of a **doll**. It is a strange story, but true.

It began on an October day three years ago ...

I can remember it clearly. The early morning sun was shining on the river when I left my house. I went to buy a copy of *The Times*, as usual.

There was a flower shop on the corner of the road where I lived. I could see the brightly-coloured flowers as I reached the corner. I turned into Abbey Lane and continued walking. I was enjoying the warm October sun.

After a few minutes, I arrived at the newspaper shop. Suddenly, I remembered that it was a **niece**'s birthday the next week. So I stopped and looked in the shop window.

doll /dɒl/ (n) a toy that looks like a small child or person
niece /niːs/ (n) the daughter of your brother or sister

30

There were games and toys, paper and pens, books and sweets in the window. 'Most of it has been in that window for years,' I thought to myself.

I almost decided that there was nothing in the window for my niece. Then I saw a doll.

She was half-hidden in the corner of the window. She was made of cloth and she had a painted face. The face was special. It had a lovely gentle look, but sad eyes.

Suddenly I felt sorry for her, sitting in that crowded window. I know that this sounds strange. But I decided to go inside and to look at her more closely.

The shop was owned by a man named Jim Carter.

'Good morning, Doctor Amony!' he said brightly, when I walked in. 'Do you want *The Times*, as usual?'

'Yes, please, Jim,' I replied. 'And I need a present for a little girl. It's her birthday next week.'

'Is it?' said Jim.

'Yes,' I said. 'I was looking at that cloth doll in your window.'

'Oh?' said Jim.

'The one that's half-hidden in the corner,' I said.

Jim looked surprised. 'That doll?' he said. 'She's a little unusual.'

'Can I see her?' I said.

'She's also very expensive,' he said.

He took the doll from the window and gave her to me – and I nearly dropped her in surprise. She was beautifully made – she seemed almost alive! Her dress and other clothes were hand-made, not made by a machine. And her face was hand-painted – I could see it clearly now.

'She's lovely!' I thought. 'She was made with a lot of love.'

I could see this love in the doll's face.

I put her down gently. 'How much do you want for her, Jim?' I asked.

'Twelve pounds, Doctor Amony,' he answered. He saw the surprise in my face and continued, 'She's expensive. I did say that, didn't I?'

'You did,' I agreed.

'Dolls like this cost as much as twenty pounds in the centre of London,' said Jim. 'But I'll tell you what I'll do, doctor. I'll sell her to you for eleven pounds.'

'Who makes them?' I asked. 'I'd like to know something about the person who can make beautiful dolls like this.'

'The woman has lived in Hardley Street for some years now,' said Jim. 'She sometimes comes into my shop and she brings me the dolls.'

'What's her name?' I asked.

'I'm not sure,' Jim answered. 'It's something like "Callamy".'

'What's she like?' I said.

'She's a tall woman with red hair, and she wears very expensive coats and hats,' replied Jim. 'But she's got a very serious face. She never says very much when she comes into the shop. I'm honestly always glad when she leaves.' He stopped for a minute and then said, 'And I've never seen her smile.'

I couldn't understand this. How could a woman like that make dolls as beautiful as these?

'I'll buy the doll,' I said at last.

Eleven pounds seemed a lot of money for a doll. As I counted out the pound notes, I felt a little silly. Yes, the doll was a present. But I knew the *real* reason for buying her – I didn't want to leave her in that shop window.

I took the doll home and put her in my small bedroom. She seemed to fill the room with her loveliness. I carefully put her into a box. Then I covered the

box with brown paper. Later, in the afternoon, I went to the post office and posted it to my niece.

In the following days, I could not stop thinking about the doll, or about the gentle face and the sad eyes. I remembered Jim's description of the woman who made her. How could a woman like that make a beautiful doll? It was difficult to believe.

So who was she? I wanted to know, but the weather got cold and wet. Children in the area became ill, and I was suddenly very busy.

I soon forgot about the woman – and the doll.

◆

One day, a few weeks later, my telephone rang. A woman's voice said, 'Is that Doctor Amony?'

'Yes, it is,' I said.

'Do you visit people who can pay for your visit?' the woman asked.

'Yes, sometimes,' I replied.

'How much does it cost?' she asked.

The voice sounded unpleasant. The woman seemed to think that money was more important than the sick person.

'A visit will cost five pounds,' I replied.

'Oh,' she said.

'But if you really can't pay, then I don't ask for the money,' I said.

'That's all right,' she said. 'I can pay five pounds.'

'What's your name?' I asked.

'Rose Callamit,' she answered. 'I live in the house next to the cake shop in Hardley Street. My rooms are on the second floor.'

'I'll be there soon,' I told her.

◆

I arrived at the house next to the cake shop in Hardley Street ten minutes later, and went up the stairs. They were narrow, dirty, and badly lit.

As I reached the top of the stairs, a door opened.

'Doctor Amony?' said the unpleasant voice.

'Yes,' I said.

'Please come in,' she said. 'I'm Rose Callamit.'

She was a tall woman, between forty-five and fifty years old. She had red hair, dark eyes and a bright shiny-red mouth.

We went into the front room. It was a cold, ugly room, and the furniture was cheap and badly made. On the cupboard in the corner were a lot of small glass bottles.

Then I saw the dolls.

They were hanging from the walls and were thrown carelessly across the bed. Each doll was different, but each one was as beautiful as my doll. It seemed impossible that this rough, unpleasant woman could make them.

Rose Callamit looked closely at me. 'You're a very young doctor,' she said.

'I'm older than I look,' I said coldly. 'You think that I'm too young. Shall I go away again?'

She laughed at me. 'You don't need to be angry, doctor!' she said. 'You're very good-looking for a doctor.'

'And I'm a very busy doctor,' I said. 'Are you the person who's ill?'

'No, it's my niece,' she replied. 'She's in the back room. I'll take you to her.'
Before we went in, I had to know about the dolls.

'Do you make these dolls?' I asked.

'Yes,' she replied. 'Why?'

I felt very sad. 'I bought one for someone's birthday,' I said quietly.

She laughed. 'And I'm sure that you paid a lot of money for it,' she said.

She took me to a smaller room at the back and started to open the door.

'Mary, it's the doctor!' she shouted.

Then she pushed the door open wider to let me in.

'Don't be surprised when you see her, doctor,' she said loudly. 'Her left leg is twisted!'

The girl, Mary, was sitting in a chair by the window. She heard the woman's words. A look of unhappiness crossed her pale face, and there was pain in her large dark eyes.

I was angry at the red-haired woman. The words were unnecessary. She wanted to hurt the girl.

Mary was not more than twenty-five years old. But I could see immediately that she was very ill. I looked again into those dark eyes.

'Something inside her is dying,' I thought.

After that first visit I always remembered the sweetness in her sad face, her poor, thin body and her dry, unhealthy hair. But something filled me with happiness. Around her were three small tables – and on them were all the necessary things to make the dolls! Brightly-coloured paints, and pieces of cloth of many different colours and shapes.

I soon understood that her twisted leg was not the reason for her illness. I noticed the way that she sat. If I was right, I could make that leg straight. I was almost sure that I was right.

'Can you walk, Mary?' I asked after a minute.

She looked at me, then looked away. 'Yes,' she answered, quietly.

'Please walk to me,' I said, gently.

'Oh, don't,' she said. 'Don't ask me that.'

I didn't want her to suffer. But I had to be sure that I was right.

'I'm sorry, Mary,' I said. 'Please try and walk. It's important.'

She got up from her chair very carefully and moved slowly towards me. I looked closely at her left leg. Yes, I was right!

'That's good,' I said. I smiled at her. I wanted to show her that I was pleased.

I held out my hands to help her. She looked up. Again, I saw the pain and hopelessness in her face. She seemed to be crying out silently to me for help. She lifted her hands towards mine – and then they fell back to her sides.

'How long have you been like this, Mary?' I asked.

Rose Callamit answered for the girl. 'Oh, Mary's had that twisted leg for nearly ten years now,' she said. 'But I asked you to come for a different reason. She's ill. I want to know what's wrong with her.'

'Oh, yes, she's ill,' I thought. 'Perhaps she's dying. I knew that immediately.'

I wanted Rose Callamit to leave the room, but she didn't. She laughed and said, 'I'm staying here, Doctor Amony. You look at Mary. Then you can tell me what the problem is.'

◆

When I finished my examination of Mary, I went with Rose into the front room.

'It's possible to make her leg straight,' I said. 'Did you know that? With help, she could walk in–'

'Stop!' she shouted loudly. I jumped. 'That's enough! You must never say anything about that to her. The best doctors cannot help her. No stupid young man is going to give her hope. If you ever do, you won't come here again. I want to know what's wrong with her. She can't eat or sleep and she isn't really working. Now, tell me. What did you learn from your examination of her?'

'I don't know what's wrong with her yet,' I replied. 'But something is slowly destroying her, I know that. I shall want to see her again, soon. I'm going to give her some medicine – it will make her feel stronger. Then I'll call again in a few days.'

'Don't say anything about making her leg straight,' she said. 'Do you understand? If you do, I'll get another doctor.'

'All right,' I said. I wanted to be able to visit Mary again, and I thought to myself, 'Perhaps, when Mary's feeling better, I can talk to her about her leg.'

I was ready to leave. I picked up my bag.

'These dolls,' I said.

'Yes?' she said.

'I thought that you made them,' I said.

'I do,' she said, in her unpleasant way. 'I draw them. Mary makes them. It stops her thinking about her leg. I don't want her to think about the fact that she'll never marry. She'll never have children.'

I walked out into the bright October sunshine. I knew that Rose Callamit was lying. I now knew the sweet person who made those special dolls.

I was happy about this, but I was also worried about Mary. I had to discover what was wrong with her. I had to know before she died.

4.1 Were you right?

Look back at your answers to Activity 3.4. Then complete the sentences about each picture.

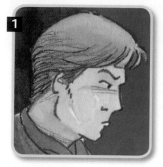

This is ....Doctor Amony... .

He buys ....

at the start of the story.

This is ....

She is the person who

....

This is ....

She is the younger

woman's ....

4.2 What more did you learn?

Write one word in each sentence.

1 Doctor Amony buys a doll for his .... niece ....

2 The present is beautiful, but it is very ....

3 Doctor Amony cannot understand how an .... woman can make beautiful dolls.

4 For many years, Mary has had a bad ....

5 Rose is more interested in .... than in Mary's health and happiness.

6 Doctor Amony thinks that he can help Mary. But .... doesn't let him.

4.3 Language in use

Look at the sentences on the right. Then complete these sentences using past passive verb forms.

> The shop **was owned** by a man named Jim Carter.
> The dolls **were thrown** carelessly across the bed.

1 The dolls ....were made............ (make) with a lot of love.

2 Their faces .... (paint) very carefully.

3 The dolls .... (sell) for £20 in the centre of London.

4 Sometimes Doctor Amony .... (not pay) for his visits to ill people.

5 Mary .... (check) by the doctor.

6 She .... (give) some medicine.

4.4 What's next?

Look at the picture on page 48 and answer the questions.

1 What are these people doing?

Doctor Amony: ....

....

Mary: ....

....

Rose: ....

....

2 How do you think they are feeling?

Doctor Amony: ....

....

Mary: ....

....

Rose: ....

....

The Doll

'Without Mary and the dolls, the money will end.' But
what was killing Mary? I still did not know.

I discovered more about Mary during my next few visits. Her name was Mary Nolan. When she was fifteen years old, she was in a bad car crash. Her mother and father were killed and Mary was very badly hurt. The car crash was the reason for her twisted leg.

Rose Callamit offered to look after Mary. The law finally agreed because there was no other person to look after the young girl. Rose always thought that Mary's father was a rich man. Then she learned that there was only a small amount of money. After that she was unkind to Mary. She made her very unhappy.

Mary was never able to forget her leg. Her aunt seemed to say: 'No man will love you. You will never get married and have children. No man wants a wife with a twisted leg.'

The years passed, and Mary began to believe her aunt. She stayed with her. She did what her aunt wanted her to do. She could see no reason to leave her aunt. So she lived an unhappy life, without hope.

Then Mary started to make the dolls.

Rose Callamit saw how lovely the dolls were. She soon realized that she could sell them for a lot of money. She was right. After she sold a few, she decided. Mary must work on them every day of the week, from morning until night.

Rose did not love Mary, but the girl produced hundreds of dolls over the years. Rose was happy to take the money for them. But now Mary was ill and Rose immediately said to herself, 'Without Mary and the dolls, the money will end.'

But what was killing Mary? I still did not know.

I could see that she was afraid of her aunt. But it wasn't that. And I couldn't ask Mary, because her aunt was always with us. Mary found it difficult to say anything to me with Rose in the room.

I did not tell Mary that perhaps I could make her leg straight. It was more important to discover why she didn't want to continue living.

I told Mary to stop working on the dolls, and I brought her some books and some chocolates. For ten days she seemed to get better.

During my next visit, she smiled at me for the first time.

'That's better!' I said. I was very pleased to see her happy face. 'You must leave the dolls alone for another ten days. I don't want you to work. I want you to rest, sleep and read. Then we'll see.'

But I could see that Rose was unhappy at these words.

When I called again, she was waiting for me in her room.

'You don't need to come any more, Doctor Amony,' she said, coldly.

'But Mary must not–' I started to say.

'Mary is much better now,' she said quickly. 'Goodbye, doctor.'

My eyes went to the box in the corner of the room.

There were three new dolls lying on top of it.

Their faces were as lovely as ever, but they had the look of death on them.

Suddenly I was frightened for Mary. I knew that Rose Callamit was lying. I wanted to push this woman out of the way and crash through the door and see Mary. But I was a doctor. When doctors are told to leave, they have to go. I still did not know what Mary's problem was. But I guessed that Rose was asking another doctor to call.

So, sadly, I left. But I couldn't forget Mary. I continued to worry about her in the days that followed.

◆

Not long after this *I* became ill. It wasn't much at first. But as the days passed it seemed to get worse. I visited a doctor friend.

'I can find nothing wrong with your body,' he said. 'Perhaps you work too hard.'

But I knew that this wasn't the reason.

I continued to get worse. I didn't want to eat and I lost weight. I began to look thin and pale. I felt tired, but I didn't sleep well at night. I sometimes dreamed that I saw Mary. She was calling to me for help, while Rose Callamit was holding her in her ugly arms.

I thought about Mary all the time. 'I wasn't able to help her,' I thought. 'She wanted me to help her and I did nothing.'

One night I couldn't sleep at all. I walked up and down my room, thinking about myself and my illness. It seemed that I was suffering from the same illness as Mary.

Suddenly I knew what was wrong. I was in love with Mary Nolan! And because I couldn't look after her, I felt ill and unhappy.

'I know why Mary's dying!' I thought. 'She's dying because nobody loves her. Nobody in the world is giving her hope for the future. Her mother and father are dead. Her aunt only keeps her because she makes money from Mary's dolls. Mary has no friends and she feels ugly because of her leg. Her life is empty – except for the dolls.

'I have to see her! I have to speak to her for a few minutes, alone – or she'll be lost to me for ever!'

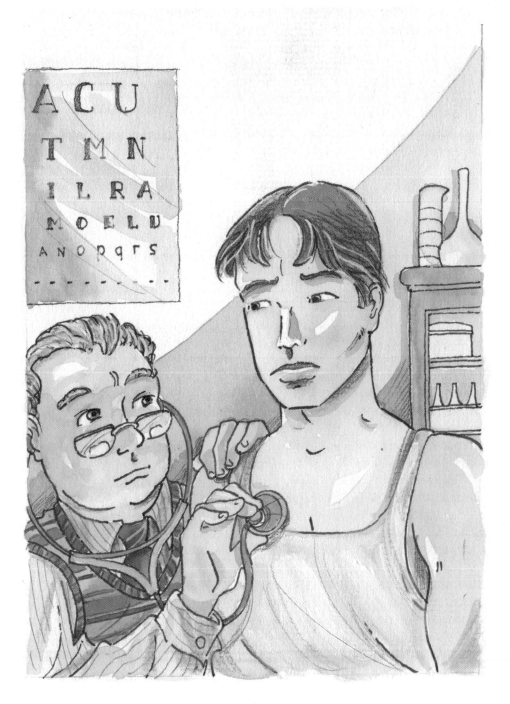

I thought about this all through the night, and the next morning I telephoned Jim Carter at his shop.

'This is Doctor Amony, Jim,' I said. 'Will you help me?'

'I'll do what I can for you, doctor,' Jim said. 'You saved my son's life last year, and I'll never forget that. How can I help you?'

'Thanks, Jim,' I said. 'Do you remember Mrs Rose Callamit, the doll woman?'

'Yes, of course,' said Jim.

'When she comes into your shop again, I want you to telephone me. Then have a long conversation with her,' I said. 'I need twenty minutes. All right?'

'All right,' said Jim.

'Good,' I said. 'Thanks, Jim. I'll remember this for the rest of my life.'

I was worried about a telephone call while I was out. So each evening I put my head round the door of his shop. But he just shook his head. There was no news.

◆

Then one day, at five o'clock in the afternoon, the telephone rang. It was Jim.

He just said, 'She's here.'

I ran to the house where Mary lived. When I got there, I ran up the stairs. Luckily, the door was not locked, and I hurried through into Mary's room.

She looked so thin now, and very ill. She still had the paints and pieces of cloth around her.

I thought, 'She wants to make one more doll before she dies.'

She looked up when I came into the room. Her eyes opened wide in surprise when she saw me. She thought that it was Rose.

She said my name. But she didn't call me 'Doctor Amony' – she called me 'Stephen'.

'Mary!' I cried. 'I've come to help you. I know what's making you ill.'

'Does it matter now?' she said, quietly.

'There's still time, Mary,' I said. 'I know your secret. I know how I can make you well. But you must listen to me while I tell you.'

She just closed her eyes and said, quietly, 'No. Don't say anything, please. Leave me. I don't want to know. The end is near now.'

I sat down and held her hand.

'Mary, please listen to me,' I said gently. 'When children are growing up, they receive love from their family. Then, when they're older, they can give that love to other people. They give love, and at the same time they receive kindness, happiness and hope. Then they have more love that they can give. But you've given your love, Mary, and you've received nothing. Now you have no love that you can give.'

I was not sure that she could still hear me. But I wanted her to live so much. I had to continue.

'It was your aunt,' I said. 'She took away all your hopes for love and happiness. And later,' I continued, 'she did a worse thing. She took away your children.'

I looked at Mary. 'Have I killed her?' I thought. 'The one person who loves her?'

Then I felt her small hand move in mine and her eyes slowly opened. She seemed almost glad to hear these words. This gave me hope.

I talked gently. I tried very hard, because I wanted her to understand.

'Those dolls were your children, Mary,' I said. 'You thought that you couldn't be a mother. So you made those beautiful dolls. Into each one you put some of your love. You made them gently and carefully, and you loved them like your own children.

'Then your aunt took each one away and she gave you nothing. You continued to use all your love. People can die when they have no love left inside them, Mary.'

I finished speaking and she moved. She seemed to understand what I was saying.

'But you won't die, Mary,' I cried, 'because I love you! Do you hear me? I love you and I can't live without you.'

'Love me?' she said quietly. 'But I have a twisted leg. How can you love me?'

'That doesn't matter to me, Mary. I still love you,' I said, gently. 'But Rose lied to you. I can make your leg straight. In a year you'll walk like every other girl.'

I saw tears of happiness in her eyes. She smiled and put her arms out to me.

I took her up in my arms and she held me. I put my coat round her to keep her warm. Then I carried her across the room.

Suddenly we heard the front door shut and the sound of running footsteps. Then Mary's door crashed open as an angry Rose Callamit came into the room.

Mary started to shake with fear. She hid her face in my neck.

But Rose was too late. She could do nothing now, and she knew it. She did not speak a word when I walked past her. I held Mary close to me. I went out of her front door, down the stairs and into the street.

Outside, the sun shone and the sky was blue. Children played happily and noisily in the street as I carried Mary home.

◆

That was three years ago.

As I write this, Mary is playing with our son. Our second child will arrive in a few weeks.

Mary doesn't make the dolls now. She doesn't need to make them. But I silently thank the day when I first fell in love with the beautiful doll in Jim Carter's shop window.

5.1 Were you right?

Look back at your answers to Activity 4.4. Then complete the sentences below.

At the end of the story, Doctor Amony takes Mary to
1 ....

Rose tries to 2 .... him, but she
can't.

Rose is very 3 .... and Mary is
4 .... of her.

But Mary and Doctor Amony are also
5 .... because they can be together.

5.2 What more did you learn?

Are these sentences right (✓) or wrong (✗)?

1 ☐ Mary's leg was hurt in a car crash.

2 ☐ Nobody was killed in the crash.

3 ☐ Mary's father left her a lot of money.

4 ☐ Rose loved Mary when they first lived together.

5 ☐ Doctor Amony tells Mary to stop working.

6 ☐ Rose stops Doctor Amony's visits.

7 ☐ Mary is dying because she has no love.

8 ☐ Mary makes dolls for her own children.

5.3 Language in use

Look at the sentences on the right. Then complete these sentences in the same way.

> I do not know **what Mary's problem was**. She seemed to understand **what I was saying**.

1 Where did he get that beautiful doll?

I wanted to know ...where he got that beautiful doll................. .

2 How could I help Mary?

I didn't know ....

3 When should I talk to her about her leg?

I wasn't sure ....

4 What was wrong with Mary?

I suddenly knew ....

5 Why did she want to die?

I understood now ....

5.4 What's next?

These people are in the next story, *The Silver Swans*. What do you think? Write A, B or C. Who:

1 ☐ works in a museum?

2 ☐ has sailed all around the world?

3 ☐ lives on a houseboat?

4 ☐ wants to live at the bottom of the ocean?

5 ☐ gets seasick?

6 ☐ needs to mend a pair of trousers?

The Silver Swans

*'I don't think that I've ever been in love.' She stopped for a minute
and then she continued: 'How will I know?'*

My name is Doctor Horatio Fundoby. But I am not the kind of doctor who
sees sick people. I am called a doctor because I have spent many, many
years studying. I studied history, and I now have an important job at the British
Museum in London.

Every Sunday afternoon I walk along a path in Chelsea, on the **bank** of the
River Thames. A lot of painters live in Chelsea. People often think that I am a
painter. I look like one and I dress like one. I have a white beard, I carry a black
wooden stick, and I wear a large, old hat. The hat is more than forty years old,
and I always wear it for my walks.

I enjoy my walks very much. There is a lot to see and hear. Boats pass on the
river. Birds cry noisily above it.

museum /mjuːˈzɪəm/ (n) a building where you can see important historical or scientific things
bank /bæŋk/ (n) land along the side of a river

52

Along this bank of the river there are some old **houseboat**s. People buy these houseboats because they like living on the water. They enjoy watching the passing boats and listening to the sounds of a busy river. They paint the boats in bright colours.

◆

One Sunday afternoon I was standing by the houseboats, looking across the river. In the deepest water in the middle of the Thames, I could see a beautiful, white sailing ship. It was called the *Poseidon*. The back of the ship was a little unusual. I knew that the owner of the ship was Lord* Struve. He was a great scientist who studied ocean life. Near the *Poseidon* were a large ship from South America and a dirty Spanish boat.

Then I noticed one of the houseboats near the bank. It was called the *Nerine* and it was very colourful. The boat was grey, but parts of it were painted in bright colours. The door was blue and the large wooden cover in the floor of the front **deck** was bright red. There were some steps going from the boat to the bank of the river. These were painted blue, like the door.

I saw a young girl trying to push back the cover. She wanted to get out, and she was halfway out of the hole, but she had a problem. She saw me. She didn't shout at me but her mouth formed the words: 'I can't open it!'

* Lord: the title of a very important man.

houseboat /ˈhaʊsbəʊt/ (n) a boat that people live in on the water
deck /dek/ (n) the flat, top part of a boat that you can walk on

I hurried towards the *Nerine*. It was sitting on the bottom of the river and I had to walk down the blue wooden steps, over the water of the Thames.

I went carefully along the deck of the boat until I reached the girl.

'The new red paint has dried and I can't open the cover,' she said.

'Wait a minute,' I said.

I used my stick to open it. A few minutes later the girl climbed out on to the deck.

She was about twenty years old. She was wearing old, blue, paint-covered trousers and a grey shirt. I thought that she looked quite beautiful.

She looked at me with big, green eyes. They were the loveliest part of her face.

'Thank you,' she said.

'That's all right,' I replied. 'I was glad to help.'

'You're a dear man,' she said. 'Do you know who you're like? You're like one of those ... older men who work in museums. Oh, I'm sorry! That wasn't very polite.' She smiled gently.

'But I *am* an old man,' I said. 'Please don't worry. In fact I do work at the British Museum. I'm Doctor Horatio Fundoby.'

'Oh!' she said. 'The British Museum!' She was silent for a second, and then she asked, 'Would you like to see my **octopus**?'

'Yes, I would,' I said, smiling.

She took me down through the blue door into a green room. I could see a small bed, bookshelves and paintings. Then I noticed two glass cases: one large and one small. In the small case were two fish and in the large one was the octopus.

'Isn't it beautiful?' she said. 'Sometimes I sit and look at it for hours.'

'Does it have a name?' I asked.

'Oh, I just call it Octopus,' she replied.

'And you? What's your name?' I asked.

After a minute she said, 'My name's Thetis.'

'Ah,' I said. 'That's the name of one of the water people in the Greek stories of long ago. Thetis was the daughter of Nereus and Doris. They lived at the bottom of the sea.'

She pulled her ear, thoughtfully. 'My real name's Alice,' she said. 'I call myself Thetis because I'd like to live at the bottom of the ocean.'

octopus /ˈɒktəpəs/ (n) a sea animal with eight legs

When she said this, I could understand the reason for her green room. It was quite dark in the room. The only lights were the ones that lit the glass cases. The paintings on the wall were in blues and greens and showed fish and other underwater animals. I was sure that she was the painter. She was almost a water-child herself, with her small nose, large eyes and pretty, short, brown hair.

'Would you like me to sing for you?' she asked.

'Oh, please do,' I replied.

'My song's called "The Silver **Swan**s",' she said.

swan /swɒn/ (n) a large, white water bird with a long neck

She sat down, closed her eyes, and sang in a sweet, gentle voice:

How shall I know my true love?
When will my true heart speak to me?
Oh, when the silver swans come sailing,
Then I will know my true love.
Then I will be with my true love,
For ever with my true love.

It was a beautiful song. But I felt that there was a sadness behind the words. The words were wise and understanding. But I knew that the young girl in front of me was never in love.

'That was lovely,' I said.

Thetis opened her eyes. 'Thank you,' she said.

'Who wrote it?' I asked.

'I did,' she said. 'It's mine.'

'Do you often write songs?' I asked, surprised.

'Only when they come into my head,' she replied.

Suddenly she moved towards me.

'How will I know my true love?' she asked, seriously. 'How will I know when I'm really in love?'

'How old are you, Thetis?' I asked.

'I'm twenty-one,' she answered.

'Have you been in love?' I said.

'No,' she replied. 'I don't think that I've ever been in love.' She stopped for a minute and then she continued: 'How will I know? Who will tell me when I am? You're so old and wise. Can't you help me?'

She looked pale and unhappy. I thought carefully before I answered her questions.

At last I replied, 'When he's ill and ugly and you can still love him. Then you can be sure.'

'When he is ill and ugly ...' she said to herself, quietly.

She sat there thinking. Then suddenly she remembered that I was there. 'Oh, I'm sorry, I'm being rude,' she said. 'Would you like some tea, Doctor Fundoby?'

'I'd love some. Thank you,' I replied.

She disappeared for two or three minutes. I looked round the room again.

At last she returned, carrying the tea things. She poured out the tea. As she lifted her cup to her mouth, she said again, 'When he is ill and ugly. Oh, thank you, Doctor Fundoby!' She smiled at me.

We talked for about half an hour. She told me about her mother and father. They also lived in London. But she wanted to live alone on this houseboat. She loved it because it was on the water. She had an evening job. But she did not tell me what it was.

Suddenly I began to feel quite ill. I wasn't sure why. But before I could decide, Thetis asked, 'Would you like to go out on deck?'

There was not much room at the back of the boat, but it was enough for the two of us. Then I saw with surprise that there was water all round the boat now.

Four dirty white swans went past us. Their feathers were dirty with oil from the river, and their eyes looked very unfriendly.

Thetis looked at them. I said, smiling, 'Perhaps they're the silver swans in your song. Perhaps you're going to meet your true love.'

She only said, 'These swans are a dirty grey silver.'

Then a small wooden boat came up to us. There was a tall, strong man in the boat – he looked about thirty-five years old. He was wearing a blue sailing shirt and dark blue trousers. He had black hair, a beard, and bright, blue eyes.

'Hello!' he shouted, and his white teeth shone against his dark beard. 'Have you some cotton to mend my trousers? I caught them on a piece of wood.'

'Yes, of course,' Thetis called back. 'If you climb up here, I'll mend them for you.'

The sailor laughed. 'I'll do it. I can't tell you where they're caught!' he said.

'Oh, I understand!' Thetis said, smiling. Then she went to find the cotton.

When she returned, she put it carefully in a piece of cloth. Then she threw the cloth into the boat.

The sailor caught it. 'Clever child,' he said. 'Thanks very much. I'll be quick.'

He moved the boat away and then tied it up next to another boat.

We watched as he mended his trousers with his back towards us. While we stood there, a large boat went past. The *Nerine* started to go up and down in the water. I suddenly felt very sick.

Thetis saw my face.

'Oh, you poor man!' she cried. 'I forget that moving boats sometimes make people ill. Come with me – I've got a bottle of medicine. It will soon make you better.'

She helped me down into the green room, and sat me in a chair. I was feeling very ill now. She went to a small cupboard and got a small brown bottle from it. She poured something from it into a spoon, and gave it to me.

'They discovered this medicine during the Second World War,' she said. 'Some of the sailors suffered badly in storms or when the sea was rough. You'll feel fine in a few minutes. Just sit there quietly.'

She went out on deck.

I heard her shout to the man in the boat: 'Hello again! What's your name?'

'Hadley. Richard Hadley,' he called back. 'What's yours?'

'I've heard that name before,' I thought. 'But I can't remember where.'

'Thetis,' she replied.

There was silence for a minute, then he said, 'Oh, that's the name of the daughter of Nereus and Doris in the old Greek stories. They lived at the bottom of the sea.'

He was silent again.

Then I heard him call: 'Where's your father?'

'He isn't my father,' Thetis said. 'He's an old man who's visiting me. He's feeling sick so I've given him some medicine.'

I heard the laugh in the sailor's voice as he shouted, 'What! Sick! On that old houseboat? It's like dry land on there.'

Another boat passed and the *Nerine* suddenly moved up and down again. But the medicine was beginning to work.

'It isn't an old boat,' Thetis said, seriously. 'It's my home. And it does move up and down a lot sometimes. You need a strong stomach.'

'Oh yes, I'm sure that you do,' he said. But I knew from his voice that he didn't really believe her.

'Really, it's true,' she continued. 'Perhaps even you'll get sick, one day.'

The sailor laughed loudly. 'Who, me? Listen, child. I've sailed every ocean and sea in the world, and in all sorts of weather – and I haven't been sick yet.'

I heard Thetis say, 'There's always a first time. Would you like to try?'

'Tell me when it gets really rough,' he said.

I heard his boat touch against the *Nerine*, as he continued, 'You're not as young as I thought. I'm sorry that I called you a child. Perhaps I'll try your boat sometime. Well, thanks again for the cotton.'

At last I began to feel better. When I went up on deck, Thetis was looking out across the river. She was watching the sailor as he went out towards the lovely, white ship.

'Oh,' she said. 'You're better.'

'Yes,' I said.

'Good,' she said. 'That medicine always works.' Then she added, 'He said some very unkind things, didn't he?'

I started to say, 'He ...'

'But wasn't he beautiful?' she continued, dreamily.

6.1 Were you right?

Look back at your answers to Activity 5.4. Then write two pieces of information about each person.

1 Doctor Fundoby .... works in a museum .... and
....

2 Thetis .... and
....

3 Richard Hadley .... and
....

6.2 What more did you learn?

Match the sentences with the pictures.

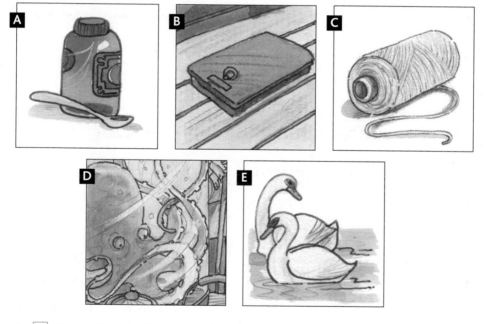

1 [B] Doctor Fundoby first meets Thetis because she has a problem with this.
2 [ ] Thetis has this as a pet.
3 [ ] She writes a song about these.
4 [ ] She gives this to the sailor.
5 [ ] She gives this to Doctor Fundoby.

6.3 Language in use

Look at the sentences on the right. Then complete similar sentences about the people in the story.

> I've sailed every ocean and sea in the world.
> I haven't been sick.

1. ...Doctor Fundoby has met... (meet) a young woman.
2. .... (paint) a cover in her deck red.
3. .... (change) her name from Alice.
4. .... (write) a song.
5. .... (not be) in love.
6. .... (make) suggestions about Thetis's love life.
7. .... (not tell) Doctor Fundoby about her evening job.
8. .... (hear) Greek stories about a woman called Thetis.

6.4 What's next?

What do you think? Complete the sentences with the right names.

| Thetis | Richard Hadley | Doctor Fundoby |

1. .... is very good at acting.
2. .... is an ocean scientist.
3. .... comes from a rich and important family.
4. .... and .... fall in love.
5. .... is happier at the start of the story than at the end.

The Silver Swans

*'He's very ill, isn't he, Doctor Fundoby? And I love him
even more then when he's well.'*

I did not see my friend for some weeks. Then, on a rainy Sunday, as I walked past the houseboats, somebody called my name.

'Doctor Fundoby! Doctor Fundoby!'

I turned round. Thetis was running up the steps from the *Nerine*.

She ran to me and said, 'Doctor Fundoby! What shall I do? My octopus has eaten one of his arms.'

I replied, 'They often do that when people keep them. Even when they feed them very well.'

'Oh,' she said. 'Thanks for telling me that. I feel much better now.'

She turned and went back to her boat. As she reached the deck, I called out to her, 'Did your sailor ever come back?'

'Yes,' she answered, and disappeared into the boat.

◆

A few days later a friend asked me to go and see a play with him. It was called *The Unwanted*, and it was at Wyndham's Theatre in London.

'There's a young woman in it – Alice Adams,' my friend said. 'She's very good, they say. One day she'll be a great actress.'

When the play started, I couldn't believe my eyes. The young actress was Thetis! I remembered, then, that her real name was Alice. So this was her evening job!

It was a sad play. Thetis played a young girl who falls in love with an older man. In the end he leaves her and she kills herself. Thetis played the part with deep feeling and understanding. It seemed to me almost that she *was* the poor girl. I cried for her at the end of the play.

◆

The next Sunday I visited her on her boat. There was now another glass case in her room. There were two large fish in it. She was sitting in front of the case, watching them. She got up to get the brown bottle. The boat was not moving much, but she gave me some of the medicine and I drank it.

'My dear,' I said. 'Why didn't you tell me who you were? I was at Wyndham's last week.'

'I did tell you,' she said. 'This is the person that I am here. This is the person that I really want to be.'

'You played the part very well,' I said. 'I cried at the end. How can you put so much feeling into the part night after night? How can you show all that pain and unhappiness if you have never been in love?'

She thought for a minute, then replied, 'That's the other side of me. I just do it.'

She saw me looking at the glass case. 'He gave them to me,' she said.

'The sailor?' I said.

'Yes,' she said.

'Where did he get them?' I asked.

'From the bottom of the river,' she answered.

'Did he? How?' I asked.

'He went down and looked for them,' she replied.

'Now I remember who Richard Hadley is!' I thought to myself. 'Does she know? And will her heart break, like the heart of the girl in the play?'

'Is he in love with you?' I asked.

'He laughs at me and says unkind things,' she said. 'Does that mean that he's in love?'

'And you?' I asked. 'Are you in love with him?'

'I don't know,' she cried. 'I don't know! I don't know! Oh, Doctor Fundoby, I hate being young!'

She put her head on my shoulder and started to cry. I tried to find the words to make her better.

◆

The next Sunday I went for my usual walk. It was very windy and the river was rough. When I saw the *Nerine*, she was moving from side to side. Thinking of Thetis, I hurried towards the boat. Her room was small and the glass cases were not safe in bad weather.

I noticed that the blue door was open, so I quickly went down the steps. When I reached the last step, I heard a deep cry from Thetis's room. I was afraid for her, and I hurried in.

Richard Hadley was lying on the bed. He was very sick. Thetis was sitting on the side of the bed, holding his head in one of her arms. His skin was a grey colour and his face was pale. At first I thought that he was dying. Then the boat moved suddenly. I understood then why he was like this.

'Thetis!' I cried. 'The medicine! Quickly! Where is it?'

'Oh-h-h!' cried the unhappy man. 'Go away, both of you, and leave me to die alone!'

'I love him!' Thetis said, happily holding his poor head in her arms. 'Oh, now I know that I love him. He's very ill, isn't he, Doctor Fundoby? And I love him even more than when he's well.'

I went to the cupboard where Thetis kept the brown bottle of medicine. It was locked. I looked at Thetis. She looked sad. 'He refuses to say that he'll marry me,' she said. Then she added, looking down at him: 'I don't mind being a poor sailor's wife. When you sail away, I'll come with you. We can sail round the world together.'

I almost laughed at her words. Thetis had no idea about a sailor's life. And she had no idea who Richard Hadley was.

The unhappy, weak man cried out: 'All right, all right, I'll marry you! I'll do anything, if you'll just go away. Please leave me to die.'

I was beginning to feel very ill myself, so I cried, 'Thetis! You cold-hearted girl! Give me the key now. How can you leave him to suffer? How can you do this to the man that you love?'

She untied a piece of blue cloth from around her neck. The key was on it. She looked at the floor as she gave it to me. I knew that she was sorry now.

As I opened the cupboard, I heard her say, quietly, 'He's sailed on every ocean and sea in all sorts of weather.'

I took some of the medicine, then I gave some to the great ocean scientist – Richard Hadley, Lord Struve.

Thetis looked at me. 'Will you come to our wedding, Doctor Fundoby?' she asked.

I was still feeling sick, and I was not happy with her. So I replied, 'If he marries you after this suffering, he's crazy.'

Lord Struve probably suddenly felt better, because he sat up. He said, 'I'm glad that you said that, Doctor Fundoby. Promises don't mean anything when they are made in ill-health.'

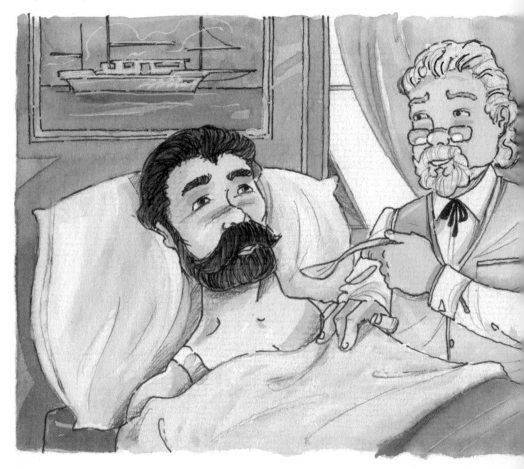

'But you wanted to come on to the *Nerine* in this weather,' she said, sadly.

The colour was returning to his face. 'I came for a good reason. I love you, and I wanted to tell you that,' he said.

'So why didn't you tell me?' Thetis asked, simply.

For a minute he did not know what to say. Then he said, suddenly, 'Because I felt ill. Now listen, Thetis. If you're going to marry me, you must know two things. You must know who I am. You must know what I do.'

'They don't matter,' Thetis replied. 'I love you.'

I was feeling better, so I said, 'And your acting?'

Lord Struve looked at me in surprise. 'Whose acting?' he asked.

'This is Alice Adams,' I cried. 'She's been in the play *The Unwanted* at Wyndham's for the last two years.'

He looked at her. 'This child?' he said. 'She *is* a child, isn't she?'

Thetis moved her head in a silent 'yes.'

But I said: 'She's England's best young actress and she's twenty-one.'

He stood up. 'Yes!' he cried. 'I remember reading something a long time ago. I've just come back from the Galapagos,' he continued. 'I haven't heard anything about England for nearly two years.'

Thetis jumped up and ran to him. 'Oh, please take me there!' she said, in an excited voice. 'All my life I've wanted to go to the Galapagos. Can sailors take their wives with them when they go?'

Lord Struve cried, 'I'm not a sailor, Thetis! I'm a —' He stopped. He found it difficult to say: 'I'm a lord.' He started again. 'I'm a kind of ocean scientist. I do a lot of my work under water. But your acting –'

Before he could finish, Thetis said: 'It doesn't matter. I never wanted to be an actress. I only do it for the money. I can buy octopuses, and live on the *Nerine*. Do you know what a good octopus costs?'

Lord Struve held both her arms. 'Thetis, can you be serious for a minute? Do you really mean that you'll give all that away for me?'

'Of course,' she replied. 'More than anything in the world, I would like to walk with you on the bottom of the ocean near the Galapagos, because ...' She stopped for a minute, thinking. 'Because I'm sure that I love you. Doctor Fundoby showed me that.'

For another minute Lord Struve held her two arms, while he looked up with a very happy look on his face. He seemed unable to believe what he was hearing.

And so the song of 'The Silver Swans' came true. Thetis, the water-child, married her lord of the sea – Richard Hadley.

◆

I still walk along by the River Thames, but I don't enjoy the walk as much as before.

Lord Struve, his wife and her octopus have gone away to a beautiful island in the Pacific Ocean. There they work together with the wonderful undersea plants and animals around them.

A family have bought the *Nerine* and they have painted her a dark brown colour. They have changed the name to the *Nelson*, after one of the greatest British sailors – Sir Horatio Nelson. I pass her every Sunday and a washing line goes from the back of the boat to the front. It is filled with washing – the clothes of small children.

And I think, as I go past, 'Do they have strong stomachs like Thetis? Or did she give them the name of that wonderful medicine in the brown bottle?'

WORK IN PAIRS.

1 **Whose thoughts are these? Match the words with the people.**

1 I was lucky. His job gave me the life that I always wanted.

2 I knew him for many years before I fell in love with him.

3 He saved my life.

4 His body was a strange shape, but he helped a lot of people.

5 When he got sick, I knew that he was my true love.

6 I was very unhappy before I met him.

7 A shopkeeper helped to bring us together.

8 I didn't want him to leave.

9 When we met for the first time, we were both in boats.

2 **Have this conversation.**

Student A: You are Fritha, Mary or Thetis, aged forty. Tell the story of your one true love and answer your friend's questions.

Student B: You are a new friend of one of the women in the stories. Listen to her story and ask questions.

3 **Discuss which love story is easiest to believe. Why?**

Complete this description for a bookseller's page on the Internet. Don't say what happens at the end of the stories. Readers will want to find out for themselves.

| Store | Books | Magazines | Bargains |

Search

❶ *The Snow Goose and Other Stories*

There are three stories in this book.

The first is *The Snow Goose*. It is about

The second, *The Doll*, tells the story of

The third, *The Silver Swans*, is about

I liked / I didn't like the stories because

You should read this book if

You will enjoy this book if

1 It is said that most people only have five real friends in their life. Do you think this is true? What is a 'real' friend? Talk to other students and make notes.

Notes

A real friend is someone who ...

You can talk to about anything

2 Where do you meet people who become friends? Make a list of the places where you have made good friends. Then talk to other students in the class. Agree the most popular place to meet new friends.

Where have you met people who became good friends?

On holiday

3 How do people become good friends? Look at these pictures from the book and some other famous friends. Choose one picture and describe to the class how they became friends. What happened next? Did their stories end happily?

4 Some people make friends through special places on the Internet. They ask you to describe yourself and the kind of friends you are looking for. Complete this form.

| GIVE GENERAL INFORMATION |

My name is ....

| DESCRIBE YOUR INTERESTS AND HOBBIES |

I'm interested in ....
....
....
....
....

| DESCRIBE YOUR PERSONAL QUALITIES |

People say I am ....
....
....
....
....

| DESCRIBE THE PERSON YOU WOULD LIKE TO MEET |

I would like to meet someone who ....
....
....
....
....
....

5 Give your book to another student and take his/hers. Nobody should know whose book you have. Then read out the last three parts of the form (but not the first part). Can the class guess who the person is?